The Big
Grayscale Colouring Book
Mallorca

Alexandra Dannenmann

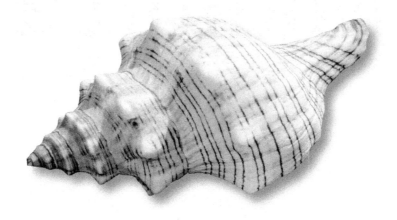

1st edition: July 2016
Copyright © 2016 Alexandra Dannenmann
Text and photos: Alexandra Dannenmann, Volker Dannenmann – Stuttgart
Translation: S. T. Paterson
www.facebook.com/AlexandraDannenmann.Kinderbuch
www.alexandra-dannenmann.de
ISBN-13: 978-1535079457

The Big Grayscale Colouring Book - Mallorca

Colour, relax and dream of holidays in the sun!

This unique colouring book contains over 45 atmospheric motifs of Mallorca, the beautiful Balearic Island in the Mediterranean Sea, just waiting to be brought to life with colour.

Each black-and-white photo is child's play to colour thanks to the many shades of grey. Whether you're a beginner or advanced, you'll be able to turn any image into a small work of art.

You'll be thrilled!

Soft pencils are best for colouring. The dark grey areas should be shaded using dark colours, and light grey areas with light colours. Subtle transitions from light to dark are achieved by using medium hues. Areas already coloured using dark shades can be retouched and brightened with light colours.

The back of each full-page photograph has been kept free, so you can cut out, frame and hang each of your creations.

Have fun!

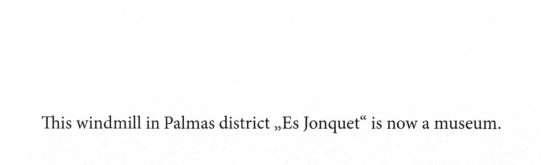

This windmill in Palmas district „Es Jonquet" is now a museum.

The emblem of Palma: the cathedral "La Seu".

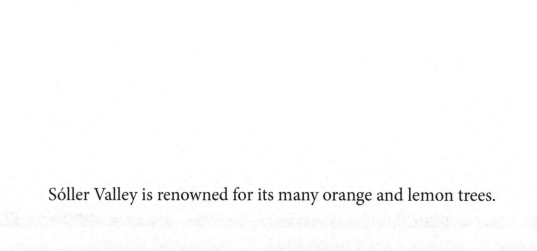

Sóller Valley is renowned for its many orange and lemon trees.

"La Lonja de los Mercaderes", the former maritime trade exchange,
is one of the masterpieces of Gothic architecture in Palma de Mallorca.
Today, art exhibitions take place in "La Lonja".

The saltworks at Colònia de Sant Jordi.

The Valldemossa Charterhouse.

Frédéric Chopin spent the winter of 1838/39 with George Sand
at the Valldemossa Charterhouse, where he composed
most of his 24 Préludes - including the famous "Raindrop".

Valldemossa Valley

Spain's most popular beer.

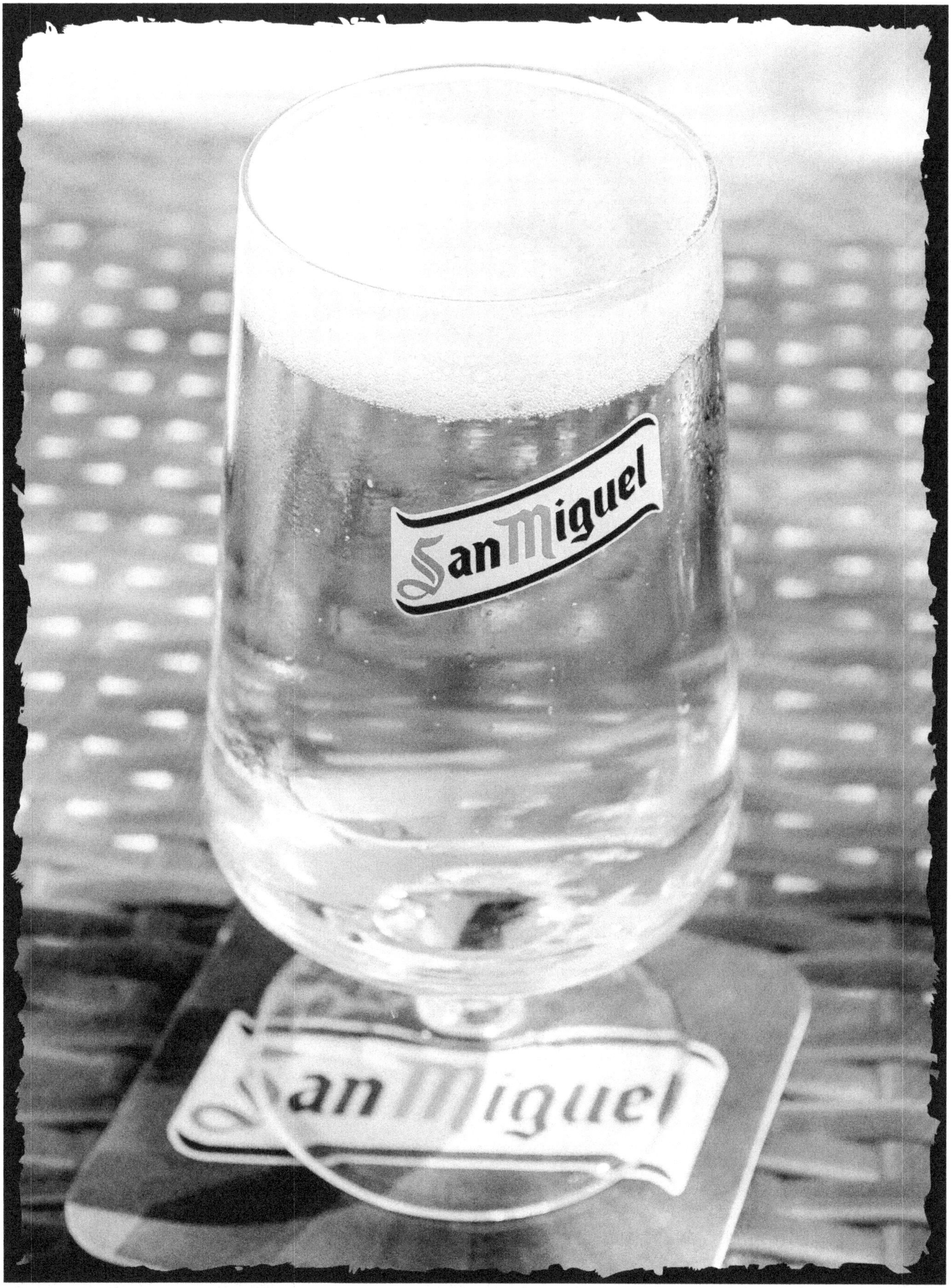
San Miguel
San Miguel

The many weekly markets on Mallorca are a popular attraction.

LENTEJAS
3,00 €
GARBANZOS
3,00 €
LEGUMBRE
"DE CARETA"
4,50 €
FRIJOLES
3,00 €
HABA PELADA
3,00 €
ARROS
BOMBITA
SA POBLA
HABAS
3,00 €
JUDIA
COCOROSA
3,00 €

Palma is home to many magnificent interior courtyards (patios).

The writer Robert Graves lived on his finca in Deià
from 1929 until his death in 1985. It was here that he wrote
his two most successful historical novels "I Claudius" and "Claudius the God".

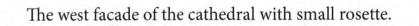
The west facade of the cathedral with small rosette.

Defence tower in Cala Pi.

Olive-growing and the manufacture of olive oil
have enjoyed a long tradition on Mallorca;
the olive tree is one of the earliest native plants on the island.

From mid January to the end of February,
around eight million almond trees bloom on Mallorca.

Portocolom boasts the largest natural harbour on Mallorca.

The most beautiful lizards can be found on
Sa Dragonera (meaning "Dragon Island").

The cathedral "La Seu" and government palace
"Palau de L'Almudaina", the official residence of the king.

The Secret of the Forest
Search for the hidden pieces of jewellery.

The forest has concealed its secret for many a long year: a splendidly decorated little box buried beneath leaves and mushrooms.

But a wily forest-dweller has discovered the key to the box - and with it the precious jewels inside.

Look for the pieces of jewellery hidden in some of the pictures, and bring the forest to life with vibrant colour.

An enchanting colouring book that helps you forget everyday life and restores inner peace and balance.

A book for discovery, for unwinding, and for dreaming.

With over 30 richly detailed hand-drawn illustrations waiting for bright and beautiful colours.

As the backs of the full-page drawings have been kept free, each motif can be cut out, framed and displayed.

Have fun!

Video review: https://youtu.be/fUl83PsXFqc

ISBN: 978-1518833953

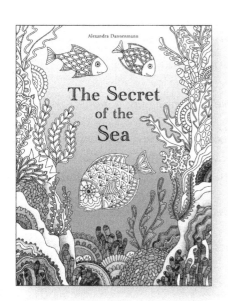

The Secret of the Sea
Search for hidden treasure from the sunken ship.

The sea has kept its secret hidden for many years: a sunken ship, loaded with the precious riches of a royal treasure chamber.

But storms and raging waves wrecked the ship and sent it plunging to the seabed.

Dive down into the depths of this enchanting water world, past exotic marine dwellers and rare water plants. Look for the treasures concealed in some of the pictures. And bring the underwater world to life with vibrant colour.

An enchanting colouring book that helps you forget everyday life and restores inner peace and balance. A book for discovery, for unwinding, and for dreaming.

With 45 richly detailed hand-drawn illustrations waiting for bright and beautiful colours.

Have fun!

Video review: https://youtu.be/vJtIIfy7sv4

ISBN: 978-1530906734

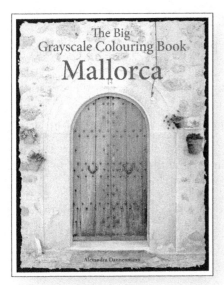

The Big Grayscale Colouring Book: Mallorca

Colouring book for adults featuring greyscale photos.
Colour, relax and dream of holidays in the sun!

This unique colouring book contains over 45 atmospheric motifs of Mallorca, just waiting to be brought to life with colour.

Each black-and-white photo is child's play to colour thanks to the many shades of grey. Whether you're a beginner or advanced, you'll be able to turn any image into a small work of art.

You'll be thrilled!

The back of each full-page photograph has been kept free, so you can cut out, frame and hang each of your creations.

Have fun!

Video review: https://youtu.be/eJC__9YqXuA

ISBN: 978-1535079457

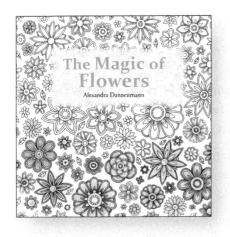

The magic of flowers

Adult Colouring Book: Flowers and Butterflies.

Forget your hectic everyday life with these enchanting floral motifs.

Find your inner peace and balance by colouring in over 30 lovingly hand-drawn illustrations: blossoms, meadows carpeted in flowers, butterflies, floral patterns and mandalas await transformation in the most stunning hues.

Let go of daily life and give free rein to your creativity.

Video review: https://youtu.be/Nthd5WGSWUw

ISBN: 978-1535079631

Find more information on my homepage http://alexandra-dannenmann.de
or Facebook page http://www.facebook.com/AlexandraDannenmann.Kinderbuch.

Made in United States
Orlando, FL
21 July 2023

35336526R10057